The Gilded Flicker

poems by

Joanna Doris Brown

Finishing Line Press
Georgetown, Kentucky

The Gilded Flicker

ACKNOWLEDGMENTS

Many thanks to the following publications, in which these poems have appeared:

"Calypso," in *Ethel Zine*
"Building Waves," in *Emerge Literary Journal* (honorable mention in (Un) civil Disobedience contest)
"I get lost in their scars (II)," previously titled "The Science of the Exam;"
"Celia," previously "Celia's Story," both in *2Horatio*
"Outcropping" in *2Horatio: Poetry of the Pandemic*
"Wedding and" in *Eclectica Magazine*
"Two Gilded Flickers Speak at the Wall," in *Chiron Review*
"Fossilized?" in *Evocations Review*
"My sister, walking down from the bimah at our aunt's funeral" in *Angel's Flight-Literary West*
"Song," previously titled "Wood Song," in *Earth's Daughters* and *bird's thumb*

I also would like to extend my gratitude to Elaine Sexton, for her expert poetry instruction and encouragement over the years and review of this manuscript.

Publisher: Leah Huete de Maines
Editor: Christen Kincaid
Cover Art and Design: Beth Braganca Bell
Author Photo: Rebecca Kislak

Order online: www.finishinglinepress.com
also available on amazon.com

Author inquiries and mail orders:
Finishing Line Press
PO Box 1626
Georgetown, Kentucky 40324
USA

Table of Contents

For Rebecca

i get lost in their scars (I)
for a moment we are swimming together

i.
when did you do this? i ask
as she lies, supine on the exam table
scars like a school of fish across her stomach
light pink, diagonal, tremulous, taut
with my stethoscope i hear bubbling gently in 4 quadrants
i swirl in eddies

ii.
do i have to wear a gown?
sleeves covered
whisper-thin lines horizontal
tiptoeing up
slender arms
suddenly the sadness, he says
i cut and-
you feel better, i say

Calypso

So lonely I've been on this island in the sea,
talking to myself and the orange-eyed violets.
Spread-beaked ravens, black skimmers roam,
and at night, I look up at my sisters—the Pleiades.

Odysseus stopped here for seven sparkling years;
then Zeus tore him away—
and I was left alone again;
I have no place but here.

          *   *

I have twined my braids into a splendid coil
checked my image in the water's mirror
but it is replaced by my father, face tight with strain
millennial dust, tracked with tears

Then across the sea, in supple
golden sandals, a stranger comes
She hugs her bronze-tipped spear to her side
asks to rest for the night

I detained her hero—
I'm afraid she will be angry with me
but she smiles, puts her finger to my lips
takes my hand

We walk to my cave
firefly lanterns, tapestries:
waterfall framed by cypresses, clustered grapes
the rocky foam-flecked shore
the sweet drip, drip from ceiling spires

I offer her my favorite nectar
she drinks thirstily
feeds me forkfuls of ambrosia
When I slide back her cloak

grey eyes flicker
Her fingernails graze my neck, she unbraids me
I have never been so hungry
My lips burn, I follow them

Caged

I.   Starry Night

Brown-haired boys, young teens,
standing inside locked metal fences.
An officer, gun at belt.
At center, young boys far smaller than
my sons, on a forest green matt
one in navy sweats, cuddled on a foil NASA
thermal near two others who recline.
Heads toward center, legs extending out:
three-pointed star. Against all, the
subtle diamond grain of wire fencing.
Cheap blankets—glowing silver—
scattered in this warehouse at the border.
Space jewels, it's time to take off.

II.   Women of Liberty

She is not interested in storied pomp
or border walls but in our masses'
huddled longing. No cries for vetting
cross her statuesque lips. Not this
welcoming majestic, inside of whom
so many have clambered up, up,
in shell-like spirals yearning for this
welcoming surround.
At Lady Liberty's foot: beautiful Therese,
legs dangling. As she rose,
my heart launched from mournful grounding
and flew, billowed by her bravery.
She is our mother and we her children.
Unite us.

grey hours

you tug at the white clip on your feeding tube the color of dust
i miss your firework stories, your commanding piano splashes
you tap out a song, left hand on knee, neat fingernails, no sound
what are you playing, Riva?
i am listening
years ago, you wanted me to sing Lieder with you
i offer to now, but you shake your head
instead my phone plays *An Die Musik*
life's mad, furious tumult
on to the sharp inventions of Bach, your favorite

Building Waves

Of the waves, stippled with tiny dark diamonds like a fish's scales
Lapping, retreating, lapping, retreating
Of my son's sandy dusting of freckles across his nose
Of his new tooth, tiny serrated edges behind the baby tooth emerging
from living gum
Of my (((name))) which would have an echo if pronounced aloud on
certain talk radio shows
(((May my name have an echo, I once thought. May my voice repeat
into time)))
Now all I want to do is stretch my skin into a shield over my children

Of punishing the sound
Of punishing the person who makes the sound
Of punishing the name that is loud but fades again and again into
nothingness eventually
Of wanting it to fade. Of wanting to fade

Try the reverse, play the echo backwards, sound waves softly lapping
retreating then lapping retreating lapping
Speak it aloud: Brown rown own wn
Can we own it? Make it n(e)w?

Of the rock that juts out by the water
Of the bronze swath across the sand like a clay tiger in a glass jar
Of the rock that begins to slip under water towards high tide

I do not hate all pregnant women

Water child, I cannot find you.
Somewhere between my speculations and walled-off enclosures

you exist.
Water child, you flowed from me in a rocky, red river—

do you inhabit now its whorls, its silty depths?
Or are you a translucent nymph, singing with the river goddess?

Before, you were a mage who made my breasts swell and harden
my back pain dissolve,

such a wondrous spell you cast.
You have left me and wracked me in pain with your passage—

I search, search for your music, your scent;
you see, I loved you so.

I get lost in their scars (II)

When he and I first met, I ran my fingers
over a red-marble cyst
that lit up his cheek.
He explored the room:

faked a layup, palmed the ceiling, played with the otoscope.
I taught him how to see my middle ear,
that shiny moonscape,
found faint, sunset stretch lines

on his pine-dark skin—biceps, back—
that rapid growth had drawn. He was from Chad Brown,
a red-brick hell-hole,
looked out for his sister.

The next year, two of my patients shot dead,
faces smiling from the front page and he
returned, four new holes
in sculpted body: thigh, flank, entry, exit.

Dressing off, dressing on. He sat still
in sotto voce reeled out a curly tale
of *henney* sprinkled with weed and *my boys*;
stolen car, war over texts and turf.

When I take down these notes I write
that he presented in *no acute distress*
or of wounds with *healthy granulation tissue*
or that *social support is recommended.*

Yet all I can see are holes,
charred, raw rims.

Outcropping

I sit at our tiny, wrought-iron table on our porch
        Over the railing, in the rectangle of yard, lilacs are nodding

Really, it is an inversion of a mask, this rectangle view
        (Lips of grass, eyes of sky)
Open wide my nose, my mouth
        Feed me air more precious than any cannula

On my street, people wear lilac masks on their faces
        but cannot mimic the spring
The bougainvillea biker & his dogwood daughter
        ease past timid cars
and the young chrysanthemum
        straggles, tilts on her wheels, rights herself
blooms forth to catch up

The lilacs mutter like gloves in a rectangular box
        empty fingers waving
Unlike the porch's glossy, framed invitation
        the gloves, the EKG machine and I must be covered
the curtains down

Flight

warm salt scent
flutter then stillness

quail
from the sea

so many
curved wings, black tufts, orange blue bellies,

knee deep encircling our campsite
we who have seen so much but never this

wade through the feathery pressing, joyous,
piling them in baskets

      after the flaky manna like dry
      rice cereal you mix with milk
      give to your five-month old

      which at the beginning was luscious
      a hint of coriander
      until the blandness

we keep gathering
through the ringing cool of night
flying stars overhead

an ache, groove, in my arm from carrying
we trudge back home, spread dead birds
out on the ground

to return later for our feast
such luxury

is there anything wrong with wanting something
you can sink your teeth into?

we had no idea
the meat would blaze
the minute it touched our lips

Wedding and

Purim, so no veils—we started behind hand-made masks.
Yours bright blue, a butterfly with glued-on jewels,
mine pink, cat's eyes, yellow feathers; and our task

in white satin pumps together to smash that glass,
leaving jagged cuts to repair, but with what tools?
During the ceremony we'd pulled aside the masks,

to open wide each other, in joy to bask.
It is the sharpness of those cuts I feel
and the soft plume of seeing, the task.

We dripped into our children who danced
in superhero masks, climbed hills and fell.
And sometimes it was a ball.

And sometimes into their rooms at night I steal
to hear them breathing. And wish to stall
their melting clocks. Skin raw beneath, we peel

away the masks. And you and I clasp, falter
like mosaic, is that the task? Again and
again, refashion the blood-kissed glass?

The Dishwasher

Metal insides gleam like knives, like the steel surface of a pond or the clean expanse of my confidence when the world is sparkling. First it was installed badly and the shelves slipped out. Now it's fixed, and you think we have to run this thing every night because it's so small. I think it's wasteful. You ran it when I'd decided not to. And I love you like a whirlpool, but not in any way that is energy efficient. No, my love spins and throws circular sluices in unpredictable spirals. And my fury is greater than a rapid cycle, my wounds deeper than the cavernous depths of any appliance. Yet in the end there is solace in your arms that circle 'round me and touch my empty pockets and corners, wash out my crumbs.

Two Gilded Flickers Speak at the Wall

Birds at Organ Pipe Cactus National Monument
on the U.S. Southern border

The organ pipes are
sonorous and won't forget.
Dusty winds still play
the tune from when we met—an
airy romp, a jittery fugue.

*   *   *

My love, walls cannot
separate us. I can perch
at the top of these
planks and see your spotted down,
meet your clear, black eyes. How lucky.

Celia

I.
Scrambling eggs for her little sister & brother,
Celia makes comparisons—here, Rhode Island,
to home, Honduras: *San Pedro Sula*,
boyfriend shattered on the sidewalk.
Her brother, Luis, crouched in the closet,
front door bashed in by a *Ponce* leader.
I don't know she'd answered, heart pounding.
Her sister, Marielis, strapped to her breast,
ate a softened carrot, tore a tortilla,
laughed at the boy waving the pistol.
Gracias a Dios, he didn't find Luis.
Her will hardened, she found a new door,
she kept them alive.

II.
The coyote eyed her hungrily, even as she felt herself grow shabby,
stretched in the border desert, jumpy from snakes,
spiders, wondering why they'd risked so much.
The sun like lava overhead, her brother's
smile loose, away from the gangs, but she slept one arm
over the water jug, the other settling Marielis close,
almost sobbing, almost yielding, hating her mother,
whose hummingbird lullaby sang in her mind
as she tripped on a diamond-back.
How could a mother leave her daughter?
The desert rattled its castanet, its hiss, and on they crept.

III.
The reunion sparkled with her mother, father, their new baby;
the three travelers refueled on food, sleep. Yet the years
away from parents, of *remesas* not *besos*—too long!
And now ICE spiders over LA, Chicago, D.C.
She slowly exhales, scrubbing dishes, steam
clouding the window, her breaths cool.
She and Luis would go to school today,
Marielis & the baby to daycare.
Her bare feet tap the linoleum—
three without papers, three with—
she envies the baby in its yellow onesie,
its red, white and blue spoon.

In spite of the mist

You and she head out on a long walk, on *shabbat*,
dragging the boys, no more lolling around indoors,
in spite of the mist, the impending drizzle
and the boys climb the rock walls that cradle
the emerald lawns, balancing, darting like cats,
the older about to leap over a break in a wall
when you stop him, the younger spots a dead bird
wing white and black plush and you warn
him not to touch ("you could catch Cthulhu's maniacal
virus" explains the older), soon the younger whines
his hip hurts so she carries him piggy-back a while,
strength a replenishing spring, at times you hold
her hand, four boots stepping in unison
other moments strides asynchronous one
bringing up the lead or rear listening to a child chatter
about the value of rare Magic cards or silent,
and the drizzle comes, so you hand out
the jackets from your pack, here you are at Wayland,
The Runcible Spoon, Red Stripe but you cannot stop to eat
and at Waterman walk downhill to the tiny park, trees bent,
underbrush scraggly, the smell like honey and you all imbibe,
and into the river, for your bodies are kayak and rower,
streamlined and knotty, strokes rhythmic,
past India Point Park, with its cement bannisters and
coiffed maples, neat benches, and as the
current sings you hug your sons and hold her

Fossilized?

for David Buckel

Early morning: can we afford to linger
on the plush pink sofa blaze of cherry
blossoms? Their dewy cry reminds me
of a young man's lips. Such flowers wake
earlier as the winters warm.
Thoughts turn to my friend, split lip,
rose bruise, from a night gone wrong—
that park was in Jerusalem.
But this is Prospect, and what are ours?
Another gay man dead. This one, I never
met, but love in pictures & papers:
the gentle tilt of chin, the cloud forest gaze,
the sea-change work that helped
an ocean of us. He chose a self-anointment:
cloying carbons soaking hair and skin,
then the sun came down to feast.

the sky

pink	against the outline of your head
	Narragansett at sunset before the flames
white	cross-country air from the West
	even my father in Philly *can't breathe, bummer*
orange	our friend huddled in an apartment
	in Eugene with her brother
red	the matte thunder blotted smudged
	against which a kangaroo leaps black cutout
inky black	at noon a viscous soup
	night/day flipped
yellow	Chateau Boswell vineyard
	triangles tinted accented stripped
purple	a hint in the tannins burnt to a crisp
	overlaid on a lavender sunset
indigo	our collective breaths
	the Earth's long forlorn sigh

My Uncle Has Lung Cancer

yesterday I was exuding spores
I felt so generous

here, have this one
it is custom designed

emeralds and rubies
but no crushed feet

craggy pits, tiny hills and valleys
and when it cracks open at an undisclosed time
worlds

one a forest green flew a hundred yards
broke into glasslike shards

the smell deep pine needles
Arthurian spirits

and here, this is yours, dry and brittle
like a tan grass in winter

it can fly 1000 miles
descend

into dust
inevitable vanishing

On the Roof

this fiddler on the roof
sounds crazy!
why does he do it?

oh, I believe he's there

and this shooter on the roof
sounds crazy!
why does he do what he does?

if he's not there
what does he mean?

*   *   *

the teacher whispers *phone call—threat*
while children around us proudly display their work
in the 2nd grade class of the Jewish school

I couldn't come to the parents' presentation the next day
so am the only parent there, learning
about African Middle-Eastern Asian animals
schoolmates come and go

looking at an Indian cheetah nursing her cub I ask
We don't think it's real do we? she shakes
her head *but Michael [the principal] seemed nervous*

my son tells me about the long-legged buzzard
who nests from country to country
and we are locked in

*   *   *

Picking my way through cucumber vines
        Their hair sharp against my ankles
[Eat a few—Isaiah, what would you do?]
Plinth, seeds brisk against tongue's flesh under this hot sun
        this refreshment [this respite]
[welcome into this *bayit,* this *sukkah,* wash your feet, rest a while]
after all I am a daughter of Zion and cannot leave this text
        [but let's remember an overrun city is not a prostitute]
        to lie down in this cucumber field
netted, propped up by bracing, rough, cabley vines
        and close my teary eyes a while
[a ravaged city is not a "harlot"—revise!]
or in the vineyard, the *gefen* weighed down with ruby globes
        to burst purple spheres with my teeth—such sweet relief
        to dance with the cedars, laughing
        [ruins are ruins]
rebuild
        [revising = survival]
dance
for lo, the leaves are not fading
        and my fiddle whines and weeps, my fiddle calls

*   *   *

I found an essay by a college classmate of mine—stating that Fiddler
on the Roof softened, Americanized our *yiddisher* Shalom Alechem.
The Russians in the tsarist regime were cruel no kind exceptions as
depicted in the musical. And Shalom did not have a Fiddler. Was
it real, then—in other words, authentic fiction, or added for the
American audience, crafted, molded to make it palatable not too
harsh on the tongue the ear? This symbol of freedom? Outside the
building, above the box? False hope?

*   *   *

The Fiddler floats before me
created by Chagall not Aleichem, the face so unusual.
Behind him, swaying on the horizon, a golden dancer—
is she the setting sun? Perhaps a gentle, flute-like breeze
ruffles the rough silhouettes of trees. The fiddler's left foot
doesn't appear to be resting on anything at all;
the right on a smokestack; and he is tremendously
out of proportion. The fiddle is gold and silent
trapped in this bow of time. All else blue and white
and black, except that face: a fauvist, forest green;
blue frizz of beard. Not quite human, leonine perhaps.
Yet in this silent frame, anchored to the roof, a rod
stands, topped by a blue maelstrom, a pinwheel, whirling
star. I wonder if this is a magician's staff, or if this super
mage requires only music to float, or our belief.

*   *   *

in the classroom
Benjamin in his Green Lantern T
tells me about the sunda
pangolin covered with slate plates
of armor hunted, coveted
in Chinese medicine
they roll into near impenetrable balls

I am dutifully curious, attentive to
lovely children,
delicate dioramas, while sirens blare
a jolt a quick flash
and police search the building
top to bottom and the children
don't know

Sandy, blue sweatshirt
talks about the Asian hermit crab
my brother had them
when I was a kid
the most vulnerable time when
they change their shells
backs like pink worms

*   *   *

the teacher almost stamped her foot
what is happening to this country
high cheek boned perfect face
sharp blue eyes the grief the powerlessness
the fury and something in me has mutated
face to face *peh al peh* with lack of fairness
need to protect my children—survival,
oh, it was always about survival
the Tsar infiltrating now as he did then
what was my answer? We can't accept it.
I am fighting with everything I have,
and we are lucky: there is no shooter
and the knocked over grave stones hurt
no one living—whereas my black friend's nephew
was shot in the head in a park.

*   *   *

The call at 9:45 a.m.
I'm on the roof with an assault weapon
But really, these days, all of us under assault
And it's difficult to ascribe fault
Shots fan from a car window like light beams
A black boy chatting in the park goes down, his mother screams
A Muslim woman bloodied on the train, scarf torn away
How I wish I could make music—please listen, stay
Black men 14 times more likely than white to be killed by guns
And above all a parent wants to protect her children, her
beautiful sons
Make sure my strings are strong
So I—we—can sing & play this song

*   *   *

He wanted the final clue in the scavenger hunt at the birthday
party to be about his middle name, Moshe. *Who led the Jewish
people through the red sea? Moshe. Follow the one with that name
inside—he will lead you to birthday cake!* Not all his friends knew
he had this name, it would require discovery. But I forgot to
add that clue, sometimes forget that he has that name, after my
grandfather who was Morris (Moishe) Liszansky who became
Murray Liss, that gallant man, that wonderful singer, who
laughed delightedly, called it a *mechayah*, when our older son,
two then, hid inside his cabinets in the apartment in Florida.
Moshe, Chagall's real name, pulled out of this whirlpool. We
hold onto names. We throw them back. We change them. We
draw them out of rivers, polished like new. They lead us through
parting waters.

*   *   *

the red leaf monkey was my favorite.
In Lev's diorama: rows of colored-in paper trees
the monkey's staunch, yet softened, crimson
hanging from a high branch
while a tiger tried unsuccessfully to reach it

*   *   *

After the lockdown I found Allan pacing panther-like
in another part of the building papered with windows
I hugged him he shook a twanging string
He said *I need to move my work to the breakfast room*
On my way out the mayor chief of police shook hands with me
News camera across the street with no one to talk to
And in the car back from school my older son said his class
covered the windows with towels
If there was a threat why weren't we evacuated?

*   *   *

in my dream you and I, my son, hand
in hand climb the narrow stairs
to the roof to see
the fiddler playing her violin
and the music floats up the sky
like creaking, narrow stairs
like proud cheetah's steps
like your graceful, freygish gait.
she has a long black coat,
this breathing stencil against the night
and her fiddling inarticulately
beautiful

My sister, walking down from the bimah at our aunt's funeral

When my sister fans her face
A shadow of death passes through space
Her eulogy wafts a cool breeze
A speech she delivered with radiant ease

New life, new life
At 38 weeks, she's ripe
Subjected to the stress
Of speaking at this mess

Laughter, precious balm
Restoring a measure of calm
Relieving so much tension
But missing the added dimension

That the fanning wasn't funny
In fact it was stunning
The scary truth
What was happening to this granddaughter of Ruth

****

A pregnant woman is not allowed at the graveside
Where trowelfuls of dirt clunk down on a box of pine
And prayers to a merciful God are stolen by wind

A very pregnant woman should not deliver a eulogy
But who else could have brought out so much joy
In descriptions of my aunt's flair for fashion
Her writing, fun and boxy; her political passion

****

I sing *El maalei rachamim*
Our mother's sister in song
Oh, how we will miss her
But we must move on

****

Shekhinah, magnanimous shade
Of cravings for shelter you're made
Covered by dancing, white, glowing letters, you must lift Ellen away

Glossy wings, mother of pearl
Flying is fun, have a whirl
Here is my sister, getting slowly sicker, not wanting to give birth today

****

When some air's displaced, other air rushes in
Does one soul's absence make room for another?
After the funeral, I followed them to the hospital
We didn't tell my mother, or father

****

Who by fire and who by water
Who by sword and who by wild beast
Who by hunger and who by thirst
Who by blood cells raging and who by a placenta clenching

****

A new cry a new name
The baby out, my sister heals
Still I reach for my aunt's presence, her tall form, her voice

Song

In the sawdust aria of noon
you will find me, nested in a bur oak's
hollow trunk, listening to tossing trees.
Away from crystal shard facts, from alarm
beeps and metronome switches, from maple
tapping of the mind, velvet fiddleheads
will unravel before me, a grey birch will
pencil secrets on scored, rolling bark.
For a while such stories will suffice
as I drink a potion of wood sorrel
and far-gone raspberries the squirrels
bring, and I will forget the time. But you,
you will arrive. My aching will flash,
a thorny curtain remembered. I'll breathe
your midnight silver hair, I'll carry you home.

Joanna Doris Brown's poetry has appeared in *Gertrude, Earth's Daughters, Chiron Review, Ethel Zine* and other publications. She is a physician and lives in Providence, Rhode Island, with her spouse, Rebecca Kislak, and their two teen sons. When she's not writing, she can be found working in an adolescent clinic or spending time with her family.

www.ingramcontent.com/pod-product-compliance
Lightning Source LLC
Chambersburg PA
CBHW022054080426
42734CB00009B/1335